Brisbane's Convention & Exhibition Centre against a backdrop of the city and the Brisbane River snaking its way to Moreton Bay.

Aerial view of Brisbane, Queensland's capital, looking south-west towards Mt Coot-tha.

A twilight panorama of South Bank Parklands' Grand Arbour.

The lively atmosphere of night markets at South Bank.

Sparkling city lights form a colourful backdrop to Brisbane's Story Bridge.

Steel and glass creates Brisbane's modern skyline.

The first light of day embraces Brisbane's central business district.

Brisbane city reflects its charm in the Brisbane River.

One of the traditional cross river ferries passes the River Queen.

South Bank Parklands feature Australia's only inner city beach.

Brisbane's Town Hall.

Twighlight falls on Anzac Square.

The city's oldest building, the convict-built Windmill.

Jacarandas add colour to the city's sub-tropical gardens.

Historic Customs House.

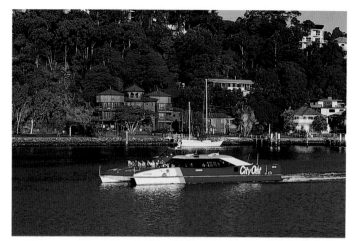

City Cats provide a high speed ferry service.

A tranquil jetty at Bulimba, one of Brisbane's many riverside suburbs.

The Riverside Markets held every Sunday offer wonderful local handcrafts.

Kangaroo Point, only minutes by ferry from the city centre, is an ideal river city location enjoyed by both tourists and residents.

The City Cat starts its day on the Brisbane River.

An early morning balloon ride.

Native wattle announces the arrival of spring for this river city.

View from the Mt Coot-tha Lookout and The Summit Restaurant and Kuta Cafe.

Historic mansions are an elegant reminder of yesteryear.

The magnificent heritage-listed sandstone Treasury building now houses the Treasury Casino.

The Mt Coot-tha Botanical Gardens.

The Gardens' Tropical Dome.

Spectacular spring blooms are a feature of Toowoomba's Carnival of Flowers, only 90 minutes west from Brisbane.

The former Botanical Gardens add a sub-tropical feel to Brisbane's skyline.

Lone Pine Koala Sanctuary enables visitors to experience Australia's unique fauna. A joey is a baby kangaroo, normally carried in its mother's pouch.

"Lone Pine Koala Sanctuary", Brisbane, *www.koala.net*

The Australian Woolshed provides visitors with a true outback experience including sheep shearing, working sheep dogs and country hospitality.

Historic Newstead House built in 1846 is Brisbane's oldest surviving residence.

A fringe of palm trees borders a flower farm at Redland Bay.

Grand View Hotel, Cleveland.

The natural wilderness of Moreton Island.

Spectacular sunset over Moreton Bay.

Tangalooma Wild Dolphin Resort beach and jetty.

Pelicans – a fish-eating bird – are very graceful in flight.

Wild dolphin feeding.

Cylinder Beach on Stradbroke Island framed by a lone pandanus.

Horseshoe Bay, Peel Island is a 15 minute boat ride from Dunwich.

Aerial view looking south-west towards Bird Island.

Sunset over One Mile boat-harbour, Dunwich, Stradbroke Island.

Brown Lake is a freshwater lake coloured brown by the Tea Trees.

Spectacular night lights of the Gold Coast Highway running through the heart of Surfers Paradise.

The crystal waters of Greenmount – one of Australia's finest beaches – are at the southern end of the Gold Coast, one hour's drive from Brisbane.

An aerial panoramic vista of the Gold Coast, set against the backdrop of the Hinterland.

Numinbah Valley's Natural Bridge.

PREVIOUS PAGE: *3000 year old Antarctic beech trees, Lamington National Park.*

Native flora and fauna of Curtis Falls, one of the most picturesque waterfalls at Mt Tamborine.

Late afternoon at the Glasshouse Mountains as seen from Mary Cairncross Park.

Noosa on Laguna Bay is a beach lover's paradise only two hours north of Brisbane with magnificent national parks and world class restaurants.

Twilight over Noosa.

Pelican Beach, Noosa River.

Mooloolaba's main surfing beach and million dollar "Loo with a view".

Peter Lik Gallery

Multi award-winning photographer Peter Lik proudly
presents his signature Galleries. The Galleries,
with their handcrafted timber floors and unique
custom decor radiate a beautiful ambience.

The stunning 'Gallery Collection' is selected from
Peter's library of over 250,000 images and hand
printed as limited edition Ilfochrome photographs.

Entering a Peter Lik Gallery is a total sensory
experience. His connection with the heart and
soul of the landscape is evident and he captures
the true feeling of the land like no other.

CAIRNS
4 Shields Street
Tel (07) 4031 8177

SYDNEY
QVB, 455 George St
Tel (02) 9269 0182

PORT DOUGLAS
19 Macrossan Street
Tel (07) 4099 6050

NOOSA
9 Hastings Street
Tel (07) 5474 8233

SAN FRANCISCO
Pier 39, Embarcadero
Tel (415) 765 7515

BOOKS BY PETER LIK

- Australia
- Blue Mountains
- Brisbane
- Byron Bay
- Cairns
- Daintree and Cape Tribulation
- Fraser Island
- Gold Coast
- Great Barrier Reef
- Port Douglas
- Sunshine Coast
- Sydney
- The Red Centre
- Townsville and Magnetic Island
- Whitsundays
- Wildlife
- World Heritage Rainforest

LARGE FORMAT PUBLICATIONS

- "Australia - Images of a Timeless Land"
- San Francisco

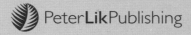